A Good Spot

by Holly Harper

illustrated by Alex Patrick

OXFORD
UNIVERSITY PRESS
AUSTRALIA & NEW ZEALAND

Chester, Tess and Gran were looking for a good spot to camp.

"This is a good spot," said Chester.
"We can swim in the pond."

There was a croak from the reeds.

"It is a good spot for frogs," said
Gran. "It's too wet for us."

They went up the trail.

"Can we camp in this spot, Gran?" said Tess. "We can pick some flowers."

There was a thump from
the weeds.

"It is good for rabbits," said Gran.
"The weeds are too long for us."

There was a hoot from the treetop.

"This is a good spot for owls," said Gran. "It's too dark for us."

Come on!

"Will we ever see the right spot to camp?" said Chester.

"This is it," said Gran.

"Wow! Look at that," said Tess.

"We can swim, pick flowers and swing," said Chester.

"This is the best spot!" said Tess.